The Garden of **GOD'S WORD**
The Purpose and Delight of Bible Study

The Garden
of
GOD'S WORD
The Purpose and Delight of Bible Study

Fran Rogers

So shall my word be
that goes out of my mouth;
it shall not return to me empty,
But is shall accomplish that which I purpose
And shall succeed in the thing
for which I sent it.
Isaiah 55:11

The GARDEN of GOD'S WORD
The Purpose and Delight of Bible Study
1st Edition

© 2016 Fran Rogers
Father and Family Books
2nd in Series
Little Books About the Magnitude of God
ISBN-13:978-0692680469
ISBN-10:0692680462
All rights reserved

fatherandfamily.com
godsgracegodsglory.com

Cover by Danielle Camorlinga

All quotes by Charles Spurgeon taken from
"How to Read the Bible" by Charles Spurgeon
http://www.spurgeon.org/sermons/1503.htm

All praise and glory go to God, for His grace and goodness in bringing me to Himself through His Word by His Holy Spirit. My thanksgiving goes to Him for family and friends in Christ who have been encouragers and supporters of His work in me, especially to Terry Adams for proofing and editing. I am indebted to Pastor Lee Lovett for his love, reverence and ministering of God's Word, and his counseling and editing.

Contents

Introduction

The Gideon Bible Society reports that 6,001,500,000 copies of the Holy Bible have been printed.

"Ranking as the world's most-read book, it has sold 3.9 billion copies. However, many more copies have been given away for free, and since it is sold worldwide it is impossible to calculate exact numbers. Since the first Bible, known as the Guttenberg Bible, written and decorated by hand in Latin in 1455, it has been translated into close to 500 languages and being translated into additional languages; the most popular version in the United States being the King James Version." Ask.com

Guinness World Records reports, "There is little doubt that the Bible is the worlds best-selling and most widely distributed book. 2123 languages have at least one book of the Bible in that language."

With so many Bibles distributed over the centuries we may wonder why those who have Bibles do not read them. And why are most people who have Bibles no happier than those who do not own one? It could be that a Bible is a gift, and the gift does not have any value to the person who received it. It may be that people who buy their own Bibles have a desire to read and learn from what they read, but some of these may put them aside because they cannot understand what they are reading"

"But, O Sirs, how the Holy Spirit casts down this imagination when He makes men feel that they are blind by nature and lets them know that the natural man understands not the things which are of God, for they are spiritual and must be spiritually discerned! A little heavenly Light suffices to reveal to men their darkness, for if they will but think, they must admit that if God deigns to teach us in the Scriptures, it must be because apart from them we are ignorant! There is no need of Revelation and the Bible is worthless; there is no need of an Incarnate Deity and Calvary is a superfluity if men already know God apart from the Lord Jesus and the Word by which He is pleased to reveal Himself! But let the Holy Spirit bring this home to a man's heart and he begins to cry out against his own pride! He bemoans his own blindness and he is quite willing to become a fool that he may be wise, a child that he may sit at Jesus' feet!" Charles Spurgeon on 1 Corinthians 10:5

If The Holy Bible is not true, then it is a lie, and effective only to deceive those who read it. If it is true, and not a lie, then it is effective to do what God says He will do. If The Holy Bible is true, then God, the creator of man, has made His Word the authority over all things, and through the power of His own being, His Holy Spirit, He commands all things. He brings to pass what He speaks in His Word through His Son, Jesus Christ, who is the Word, the Truth, and true Life. Those who are drawn to His Word and Jesus Christ know the truth working in and through them, now and forever.

Update: Since beginning this project of publishing four of our books, I have committed to donate the majority of profits from sales of our books to charity and missions. Any who purchase a book will be a participant in this vision of Father and Family Books. Visit our website fatherandfamily.com for more details, and to leave your email address if you would like to receive updates on what we are doing, and news of other publications.

Fran

Preface

My desire in writing this second book in the series *Little Books About the Magnitude of God* is to encourage, and to stir up a new interest among God's people for His Word. It is my prayer that the Holy Spirit will incite a zeal for God's Word that we as God's people so desperately need. It is the written Word that speaks of Jesus Christ, the living Word. It is the language, the vocabulary and dialect for a select people to whom God gives His Spirit for interpretation.

As a young wife and mother, with my own set of rules and troubles, I tried many sources to find help for answers in my life. I studied psychology, and in my own way, tried to be a philanthropist, thinking that I might be able to help myself, and others obtain a secure and happy lifestyle. I studied the core beliefs of other religions besides Christianity, the only religion that I had known as a child. But, in all my efforts I could never see how I or anyone else could really be happy.

I had two older Bibles, one from my childhood, and one I had as a teenager. I had memorized some parts of the Bible from Vacation Bible School (which have to this day stayed with me). But it held no particular interest for me until I came to the end of my search from other sources. I prayed for understanding as I started to read. You may notice that I am relating all this from times past with the personal pronoun "I." After several years of reading through the Bible with a schedule, things from different books of the Bible began coming together and forming patterns. Like a jigsaw puzzle, pieces began to fit, and things written centuries ago began to make sense, becoming relevant to this age, even as it was when it was written. The Old Testament and the New Testament started to compliment each other.

My interest and zeal led me to teach youth Bible Study; years later to write curriculum for youth Bible Study and Discipleship groups. Afterward, I taught women's Bible Studies. But nothing really changed in my life from these activities. It was years later and during the time of my studying and teaching that conviction came with knowledge that "I" was not a true Christian. The knowledge through study and teaching was in my mind, but not in my heart. The *light of the knowledge of the glory of the Lord in the face of Jesus Christ* did not come on until after I stopped teaching. My studies continued, knowing that the "first love" John had written about to the church in the book of Revelation had not been my first love. There was nothing of the reality of the new birth of the Spirit in me, about which Jesus told Nicodemus in John 3:3-8. I had answered an altar call and been baptized at the age of eleven, but that was not a true conversion to a new life; it was only a following of what others were doing. Years proved that that was not an effective action on my part.

Examples

There is only one memory of anyone I knew that treasured a Bible; my paternal grandmother. Everyone that knew her acknowledged that she was a Christian. Her life witnessed to it; she verbally witnessed of Christ, and could witness of God's Word against any other religious belief. It is told that she welcomed Jehovah's Witnesses and Mormons into her home so that she could witness to them. She must have prayed for me all those years before God put His witness of Christ within me.

In my seventy-six years, with much hearing, reading, meditation and memorization, the Bible has proven to be a transforming power. Jesus Christ, the living Word, is revealed from cover to cover in the written word that Christians ~ the followers of Christ ~ believe is God's Word. It has been a proven authority to change lives.

As the apostle in 1 John 5:10 says, "He that believeth on the Son of God hath the witness in himself: he that believeth not God hath made him a liar; because he believeth not the record that God gave of his Son."

No one is able to accept the Bible as the truth of God without faith, and the faith that is required is not a faith that we can conjure up on our own, but one that comes from hearing the truth of God's Word ~ *the hearing of faith.* (Galatians 3:5)

God brought me to His Word by His own Spirit, before I believed, and in His timing, through the authority of His word by the power of His Holy Spirit, He enabled me to understand my own sinfulness and my need for salvation through Christ. With continual study, the revelation from His Word brought about the reality of a *new heart and a new spirit*, giving me a new life in Christ. This life has been nourished daily for these twenty-two years, by Christ, the living Word, and the pouring out of His Holy Spirit in this new heart and spirit, and my whole life. He is continually sustaining me as He is writing His law on my mind and in my heart.

The greatest work that God does in our hearts and in our minds happens when we daily meditate and memorize the Scriptures. In the chapters ahead we shall look at how God uses His Word to work His own power in our hearts and lives. These are not the miracles that most people think of, but the supernatural working of His Spirit to change us and prepare us for the eternal glory that is promised to all His children. It is a work that proves that all power belongs to Him and not to us. Paul speaks of this in his second letter to the church in Corinth.

But we have this treasure (the light in our hearts) *in jars of clay, to show that the surpassing power belongs to God and not to us.* (2 Corinthians 4:7) We will look closer at this in Chapter One.

Come with me through the following pages and discover a new way of looking at the Holy Bible; to see it for the treasure that God meant it to be as He has preserved it. I pray that you will discover the power-changing substance that is in God's Word, and be drawn as never before into the life of Christ that is given to those who plunge headlong into the depths of the truths that are found there.

You will notice that each chapter title has within it the word "form." The purpose of God's Word will be explained in each of these chapters, from *inform*ing each person individually, to His *perform*ing His own word in and through the life of Christ's church, to see that it is all God's supernatural work. Just as He at the beginning formed the earth, and from the earth formed a man, and *breathed into His nostrils the breath of life,* God is still in the business of forming men into His own image. If you find repetition in this little book, consider that God, throughout His Word repeats Himself so that we will know what He wants us to remember.

The point of God's providing and preserving this book called The Holy Bible, is that we have the means to know Him, and in knowing Him, understand, desire, and learn how He makes us His image-bearers.

This is the end purpose for His Word, through which man realizes his chief end of *glorifying God and enjoying Him forever.* (Shorter Catechism)

Gracious Father in heaven, who am I, to attempt such a task as this? Unworthy, and incapable, there is in me nothing to accomplish what you desire, but knowing this, always brings me to you. To think of writing about you, your wisdom and knowledge, is overwhelming, almost to the point of immobilizing my efforts, but it is you who calls and you who makes a servant and supplies him with what is needed. Guide me, as one of your children, one of your sheep, with your counsel, word for word, sentence for sentence, paragraph and chapter, to the end that it will be for your glory, having only your signature. Speak to the hearts of your servant who writes, and to those who read, as only you can. In Jesus' name I pray. Amen.

Almighty God, your word is cast,
like seed into the ground.
Now let the dew of heaven descend
and righteous fruits abound.

Chapter 1

To Inform ~ Revelation

For God, who commanded the light
to shine out of darkness,
hath shined in our hearts,
to give the light of the knowledge
of the glory of God in the face of Jesus Christ.
But we have this treasure in earthen vessels,
that the excellency of the power may be of God,
and not of us.
2 Corinthians 4:6-7 KJV

The apostle Paul wrote these things to the church at Corinth using the contrast between light and darkness, and between the Creator and what He created. With these contrasts we see in one a need, and the other as able to give what is lacking. Only God is able to fulfill the need in what He has created.

Nothing can be seen in the dark. Nothing God created would have been visible if He had not first given us light. He would not need the light, but His creatures would. He is light, Himself. This same eternal light is compared to a treasure when shined into the human heart. It is a special, supernatural light, that only God can produce from His own being, that provides us with the knowledge of Himself and His glory. Paul is identifying this *knowledge of the glory of God* as it is revealed in His Son, *Jesus Christ.*

In a recent prayer our pastor prayed that the Lord would inform our consciences. I had never heard of God's Word described in this way.

As we begin with our need to be informed, and for the work of the light, we will look at the *source*, the *substance*, the *structure*, the *stability* and the *sufficiency* of God's written word.

The Source

The first verses of the Bible sum up what we need to know first. God, in the beginning created the heavens and the earth, then filled the heavens and the earth, according to His own will and word. *He spoke and it came to be; he commanded, and it stood firm.* Psalm 33:9 (Compare Hebrews 1:3 and 11:3)

When we come to God's word it must be our intentions first of all to find Him. We may see the glory of God in what He has created; but we need more than what the human eye can see. God is Spirit (John 4:24) and He reveals Himself through His written word and through His living word, Jesus Christ. They both come in the same word, the same book.

We read in John 1, *In the beginning was the Word, and the Word was with God, and the Word was God,* explaining in this first chapter that Jesus was God.

Jesus instructed His disciples, "Seek first the kingdom of God and His righteousness," *and He will provide within the context of His kingdom and His righteousness what we need in this life.* Matthew 6:33 *(paraphrased and italicized).* This was in reference to man's anxiety about this life. When we approach Bible study for our own purposes we will leave empty, frustrated, and uninformed of what we need for the heart and the spirit. God must be the first, foremost, uppermost, ultimate, and bottom line reason for our study. He alone, by His Spirit, can put within us what He knew we needed when we were created. He is the source of all of life from creation to its end and we can only know His purpose for each of our lives as we seek Him, His kingdom and His way for life.

The Substance

As the source, so is the substance that comes from the source. It is holy, therefore its title, *The Holy Bible.* Unless we understand the meaning of holiness we will fail to understand God's word. We must see it as a writing that is set apart, sanctified, unlike any other book ever written.

It is His written will, His last will and testament, the revelation of a legacy that is unknown to most. It must be opened and examined, word for word. It is powerful in itself because it was written *by the finger of God.* (Exodus 31:18)

People will say that they cannot understand it. That is true, even a believer has no ability of his own to comprehend what God says in His Word (1 Corinthians 2:6-13). It is basically a foreign language from a different world, and of a substance unknown to man. The Holy Spirit, the same Spirit that gave it to the writers, must interpret it.

For the prophecy came not in old time by the will of man: but holy men of God spoke as they were moved by the Holy Ghost." 2 Peter 1:21

"There is an interior reading, a kernel reading—a true and living reading of the Word. This is the soul of reading; and, if it be not there, the reading is a mechanical exercise, and profits nothing. Now, beloved, unless we understand what we read we have not read it; the heart of the reading is absent." Charles Spurgeon

The same source, the same substance of God's Word is of the same Spirit that works to inform those who take it in hand with the desire to know and learn what God has there for them. The light of what God wants each of us to know is hidden in His Word. The Spirit moves what is written from the pages into the mind and heart.

We must ask the question, "What good is a Bible if you don't study it and *hide it in your heart?"* It seems that just reading the Bible is like reading the label on a container of food, without opening and eating the contents of what the label describes. God's Word is a supernatural substance outside our being that must be taken in as our spiritual food. It is a requirement for a life-sustaining existence.

Jesus, when He was tempted in the wilderness used Old Testament scripture to refute the devil and his temptations.

His first quote in Matthew 4:4 was from Deuteronomy 8:3,

Man shall not live by bread alone,
but by every word that comes
from the mouth of God.

To say that we don't need to study God's Word is to say that we do not need to eat. Simply hearing it preached is like hearing an advertisement about food but never experiencing the fullness of it. Simply reading through it every year is good, but does not sustain the nourishment that is needed for spiritual life. Food to the spirit and soul is an eternal sustenance that provides more than any physical food can give to the body.

Before His crucifixion Jesus impressed upon His disciples the need to hear, remember and to digest His words. He said, *It is the Spirit who gives life; the flesh is no help at all. The words that I have spoken to you are spirit and life.* John 6:63

The Structure

The structure of what is known as God's Word, from God as the source, is based on His plan. The blueprint of this structure was taken from His image. His plan was to create in man the image that He wanted. When He said, *Let us make man in our image, after our likeness,* He meant for His character to be seen in a human form. From Genesis 1:26 we then read, *So God created man in his own image, in the image of God he created him; male and female he created them.* He meant for His character to be seen in both of these roles.

In Genesis 2:7 we read how He did it ~ *then the Lord God formed the man of dust from the ground and breathed into his nostrils the breath of life, and the man became a living creature.* From his rib God formed the woman and brought her to the man. (2:23) It is God's Spirit that was given as life to the first man, a perpetual Spirit that has continued to all generations. Though His Spirit continues to give life to all His creatures this image was marred by the disobedience of the first man, Adam. We will take up this thought in the next chapter.

This true image that God had planned for man is revealed throughout the New Testament in the person of His Son, Jesus Christ. When we study we come to understand that His Word is the means of putting into His creatures a form of words and thoughts that brings His desired results. These come from the outside into the minds and hearts of men as a means for the structure that He has planned.

For examples of *revelation* by way of *information* let's think of other books that we study. My husband, my son, and daughter all have college degrees. They each attended institutions to study for what they wanted to become. The books they read, studied, and portions memorized, informed them with the knowledge they needed. What they studied served to form within them what they were looking for. The substance within what they studied was sufficient to carry them through their courses and make one an industrial engineer, one an attorney, and the other a physical therapist.

The source, and the substance were what were needed to form the structure for each of their careers, and the building of a physical life that produces an income for this life.

We may not know all that God intends for us when we begin studying His Word. This is His time of revelation to us, as we become informed through the knowledge of His Word. Careers are established in this life through different sources, through childhood experiences, friends and family. As we gain more knowledge through our Bible study God will form His will for us, in us and through us. He will begin to bring glory to Himself through His revelation of Himself to us and in us. It is in His own power that He through His word makes us what He wants us to be.

Beginning with the Old Testament, even through the four hundred years of silence, God, through His creatures, wrote and formed a canon that has been used by His people. Adding the New Testament when prophecy had been fulfilled in His Son, Jesus Christ, the volumes were put together as one voice for His kingdom here on earth. We have a sure place to go for the revelation that we need.

The Stability

It is an imperishable source, substance, and structure. What other book, what other wisdom and knowledge has lasted as long as The Holy Bible? Written copies have been destroyed, but by God's own working He has sustained it for us. It has been written time and time again. It has been handed down verbally from generation to generation. It has been passed down, copy by copy.

For all flesh is as grass, and all the glory of man as the flower of grass. The grass withereth, and the flower thereof falleth away; But the word of the Lord endureth for ever. And this is the word which by the gospel is preached unto you. 1 Peter 1:24-25 KJV

In saying that His disciples would *know the truth, and the truth would set them free* Jesus was pointing them to the only reliable source for freedom and power. The knowledge of the truth found in the Word has not changed since the beginning of time. Men will take it and try to rearrange the words or interpret it according to their own understanding, but they can never change God, or His truth. Twisting the words only brings them under the wrath of God and His judgment. Though there may be what seem to be controversies in the written word of God, we can find the surety of all that He wants us to know when we continue to study and compare different passages and references. We look for the main things, praying that He will lead us into all the truth, even in the less important things in which we may seemingly find contradictions. Many have voiced their doubts as to the reliability of the Bible based on their findings. These want to divert attention from the main point of God to the things they do not understand. The more we study and trust God to lead, and reveal Himself, the sooner we come to trust Him in and through whatever parts we read. When we depend only on men's interpretations we are missing much of what God, our heavenly Father has for us as His children. Theologians, pastors, and teachers are meant only to point others to His Word, so that He can speak to each one personally. Too many have become public Bible gurus, and their followers only know what they have taught them. We will speak in the last chapter of the duties of these leaders, pastors and their churches.

The stability of the written word of God is based on His power and will. From the beginning of creation, through the fall that occurred by Adam's and Eve's disobedience, He has sustained all things through Christ, *by the word of His power.* (Hebrews 1:3) The apostle Paul speaks in Romans 1:16 of *the power of the gospel unto salvation.* The authority of God's Word by the power of His Holy Spirit is effectual to, in, and through those who believe. And no human is able to initiate his own belief system; faith is not of our own doing, (Ephesians 2:8-10) but through His Word and Spirit, He draws us to it, informs us, revealing in us what He wants us to know.

The Sufficiency

The writer of Hebrews speaks of the rest in Christ to which He brings us by His Word and Spirit.

For the word of God is living and active, sharper than any two-edged sword, piercing to the division of soul and of spirit, of joints and of marrow, and discerning the thoughts and intentions of the heart. And no creature is hidden from his sight, but all are naked and exposed to the eyes of him to whom we must give account. Hebrews 4:11-13

Only as we study His Word does He reveal what is in our own hearts, and through the same medium bring us to regeneration of faith and repentance of what He reveals of our thoughts and intentions of our heart. Our striving to enter God's rest is in the power of His Word and Spirit, not our own.

Its Light and Truth

The light that God, by His Holy Spirit, shines in our hearts is the light of His truth. It is His light and His truth to which He brings us to trust Him to reveal Himself and what He wants us to know about Him and ourselves. It is a delightful thing to learn of Him, and a burdensome thing to know the truth about His creatures; but that is the purpose of the light and the truth ~ to deliver us from the burden. It is through our study of the truth that works the truth of God in us. This is the power that we will talk about in the following chapters.

```
                    LIGHT
                     /\
                    /  \
                   /    \
                  / TRUTH \
                 /        \
                /          \
               / GOD'S WORD \
              /              \
             /   KNOWLEDGE    \
            ————————————————————
```

As we begin this treatise let me encourage you, according to this diagram, to look ahead, past where you are now. Think of the upper point of this triangle as where you want to be, where God wants you to be. The bottom line is a fine line, the separation of God from the world. Within the boundaries of this triangle are the knowledge of God, and His kingdom. By taking in hand a copy of His Word, we step across the line into a realm that is not yet discovered. By taking one step at a time, one day at a time, we are drawn in truth closer and closer to the light. As the light of His Word draws us closer the truth will become clearer. The path will become narrower as we are drawn closer to the light and as we learn more and more the difference between God's kingdom and the world. In the process we begin to discover the freedom of which Jesus spoke.

God's Covenant of Grace

As we study God's Word we soon come to understand that He relates to man only by covenant. His whole word is written as a covenant to His people. He initiates by creation and redemption; He provides the promises, the conditions, the requirements, and the power of His covenant.

"Man by his fall having made himself incapable of life by that covenant (the Covenant of Works), the Lord was pleased to make a second, commonly called the covenant of grace: wherein he freely offered unto sinners life and salvation by Jesus Christ, requiring of them faith in him, that they may be saved, and promising to give unto all those that are ordained unto life, his Holy Spirit, to make them willing and able to believe." Westminster Confession

Losing Ourselves

The ultimate end for our study is that we are moved into this realm of God's Word and presence so as to lose ourselves. Jesus said to His disciples, *For whosoever will save his life shall lose it: but whosoever will lose his life for my sake, the same shall save it.* Consider those who never open God's Word, those who never venture through the narrow gate that leads into the knowledge of eternal life. These are on the broad path that leads to destruction. (Matthew 7:13-14)

Andrew Murray in his book *Humility ~ The Beauty of Holiness* speaks of the *mystery of grace* that is revealed to the point of *losing ourselves in the overwhelming greatness of God's redeeming love.* Those who seek with all the heart what He has for us as His children experience this mystery unveiled.

Grace and peace be multiplied unto you through the knowledge of God, and Jesus our Lord according as his divine power hath given unto us all things that pertain unto life and godliness through the knowledge of Him that hath called us to glory and virtue; by which he has granted to us his precious and very great promises, so that through them you may become partakers of the divine nature, having escaped from the corruption that is in the world because of sinful desire. 2 Peter 1:3-5

'It is the spirit, the real inner meaning, that is sucked into the soul, by which we are blessed and sanctified. We become saturated with the Word of God, like Gideon's fleece, which was wet with the dew of heaven; and this can only come to pass by our receiving it into our minds and hearts, accepting it as God's truth, and so for understanding it as to delight in it." Charles Spurgeon

Other References for Study:
(Matthew 7:8; Matthew 24:35; John 15:16; John 1:1-5, 14, 16-18; John 6:63; John 8:12; 1 Corinthians 2:6-13; Galatians 2:4-5; Colossians 1:15-17; 2 Timothy 3:16-17; Hebrews 4:12)

Chapter 2

To Reform ~ Regeneration

Where there is no revelation,
the people cast off restraint;
But happy is he who keeps the law.
Proverbs 29:18

When we step into this realm of God's Word, seeking knowledge that only He can give, we find that there is a controversy between Him and His creation. He informs us that we are deadly creatures, having decided to live on our own, without His counsel. We learn that the human race that He created lives in rebellion against Him. Those He created in His own image rejected that image from the beginning. In the first few chapters of Genesis we see the first man and woman disobeying His first command. Within the confines of a beautiful garden God had created for Adam and Eve, God's archenemy convinced them that God was a liar.

Distorting the Truth

The adversary twisted the simple command that God had spoken. Satan made the words *of the tree of the knowledge of good and evil you shall not eat, for in the day that you eat of it you shall surely die* sound stupid to them. So they believed the enemy instead of God, their creator and provider. God's Word was thrown out of their vocabulary. They thought that they could live on their own without Him. But, they proved God to be true to His Word. He had warned them of what would happen if they disobeyed and ate the forbidden fruit. He said that they would die as a result of their disobedience. Physical death did not happen immediately, but they and every subsequent generation experiences this death. A spiritual death occurred from that point for all humanity. And while we each live here we are miserable creatures because of disobedience. Sin, which is lawlessness before God, is the nature of all who are born into this world. All are enemies of God, because all are born with the same nature as the archenemy. All this is the bad news that we learn from the beginning about God and ourselves.

The Israelite Nation ~ The People of God

In the Old Testament we learn that God chose to work through a special nation. To Abraham, his son Isaac, and his son Jacob, and through Moses, God revealed His instructions. He provided for them His own laws, with promises for blessings and curses; similar to those he gave Adam and Eve. But these were more prominent, spoken and written for them, so that there was no doubt as to their meanings and consequences. Still, within this nation under Moses' leadership, we see the same nature of unbelief and rebellion.

We see many examples of their disobedience, of God's chastisement and His leaving them to themselves to reap the consequences. Psalm 107 speaks of these times in the history of God's people.

Some sat in darkness and in the shadow of death, prisoners in affliction and in irons, for they had rebelled against the words of God, and spurned the counsel of the Most High.
Psalm 107:10-11

Without the direction, and protection through His counsel, they were afflicted; He had promised this affliction if they did not stay close to Him, and *therefore brought down their heart with labor; they fell and there was none to help.* Vs. 12

At this stage *they cried unto the Lord in their trouble, and he saved them out of their distresses.* Vs. 13

Psalm 107 speaks many times of their rebellion, and God's saving them – verses 7, 14, 20, 30. Each of these verses is followed by the same statement, "Oh that men would praise the Lord for his goodness, and for his wonderful works to the children of men!"

Deformity

In our depraved nature there is a stark difference between God's character and ours, though we are all made in His image. We, as His creation are in constant need of His presence and guidance. When

we refuse to accept, acknowledge, and receive His
Word as truth, we remain **misinformed** by Satan's
lies and His image remains marred. The **deformity** is
so great that most of the world looks the same; and
we don't realize that we are like everybody else.
Oswald Chambers reminds us that there is no
"normal" in the world. All that we see and know of
man is "abnormal." **Such is our state of deformity,
but even through this, God planned for a
restoration**.

Delight in the Law of God

*Blessed is the man who walks not in the counsel of the wicked,
nor stands in the way of sinners, nor sits in the seat of scoffers;
but his delight is in the law of the LORD, and on his law he
meditates day and night.* Psalm 1:1-2

We may be confused when we read the Psalms, one
of the most read and studied books of the Bible. It
speaks of those who are righteous; yet the Bible
teaches that *there is none righteous; no not one.* (Romans
3:10) Since the fall of man all are condemned in
God's sight as ungodly, unrighteous before Him. The
whole book of the Psalms speaks of the two classes,
the righteous and the unrighteous.

In Psalm 1 the unrighteous are described as
ungodly, *sinners*, and *scornful*. Then we see a different
nature of one who is righteous. They have a delight
in the law of God and meditate in this knowledge of

God day and night. We see a difference in those who have no knowledge of, or interest in God.

The Psalm continues in the third verse to describe the effect of this delight and meditation in the law of the Lord.

He is like a tree planted by streams of water that yields its fruit in its season, and its leaf does not wither. In all that he does, he prospers. Psalm 1:3

It is not the person's work, but the work of God's Word within the heart of the person that affects the whole life. It is the blessing to those who are within the path of the knowledge of God, through His Word, that produces the fruit.

This is where God's Word is the power in those who study. We learn that we cannot be righteous on our own. Since the fall of man, when in disobedience to God's Word Adam and Eve were expelled from the garden, all mankind has fallen from the purpose for his creation. Man no longer could claim the image of God, because of disobedience. No one was righteous before Him. Until He sent His Son, Jesus Christ, the only righteous one, there remained the need for regeneration, a reforming of a new heart that would work faith in God's Word and obedience to Him. Let's look at this regeneration from two points; first that it comes in the person and work of Jesus Christ for us, and second that it comes into a new heart given us by His Spirit through a promise given in His Word ~ *new wine in a new wineskin.*

His Righteousness for Our Sin

For our sake he made him to be sin who knew no sin, so that in him we might become the righteousness of God.
 2 Corinthians 5:21

We have no righteousness of our own, but we are given His righteousness as a gift of love from God. Our faith in His taking the punishment for our disobedience upon Himself, and dying for our sins, is the appropriation of His righteousness to us. But, it is not our faith that brings us to Him and saves us. Jesus' perfect life and His sacrifice alone is God's means of reconciling us to Himself. (2 Corinthians 5:19)

The Promise

And I will give you a new heart, and a new spirit I will put within you. And I will remove the heart of stone from your flesh and give you a heart of flesh. Ezekiel 36:26

Reformation takes place by His own power in His own timing, for regeneration, that time when we know that we have a new heart, and new spirit, and a new life. The Holy Spirit works in the new heart and spirit to bring us to repentance and faith. The apostle Paul wrote about this faith by God's grace in his letter to the early church.

For by grace are ye saved through faith; and that not of yourselves: it is the gift of God: Not of works, lest any man should boast.
For we are his workmanship, created in Christ Jesus unto good works, which God hath before ordained that we should walk in them. Ephesians 2: 8-10 KJV

It is through His Word that the Spirit of grace works in the heart of those who stay in His Word, seeking to know, love and please Him. The *obedience of faith* is what He is after. (Romans 1:5, 16:26) The power of His Word and Spirit do the work as we continue in His Word.

Experiencing the New Birth

A newborn infant cannot in this life rejoice in the experience of its physical birth; neither can it at any time remember that day or time. The record of a baby's birth is filed in the county and country in which it is born. The parents and others who love this child will remember its birth in years to come.

Jesus told Nicodemus, a religious leader of His day, "Truly, truly, I say to you, unless one is born again he cannot **see** the kingdom of God." John 3:3

Truly, truly, I say to you, unless one is born of water and the Spirit, he cannot **enter** the kingdom of God." John 3:5

When we read and study the third chapter of John we come upon truth that was spoken by Jesus Christ to one who knew the law, who taught the Scriptures from the Old Testament, yet he was no better off than the newborn infant. We are born blind and cannot see spiritual things. We cannot understand this life, nor any that is to come. We are deaf and helpless to know the things of God. We do not understand truth because it comes from God only through the revelation of His Son, Jesus Christ.

When Jesus prefaced His statements with the words *truly, truly* (verily, verily in the KJV), He was bringing attention to the truth that followed, though

Nicodemus could not understand it; and he had been brought up with the Law and the Prophets. He knew of Ezekiel 36:26 and the promise *to take away the stony heart* and replace it with *a heart of flesh*.

The writer of Hebrews quoted the promise, *I will put my laws into their minds, and write them on their hearts, and I will be their God, and they shall be my people.* (8:10). When He puts within us the new heart and spirit He has a new tablet on which to write and record His law and promises, so that they will not be forgotten, and through which His Spirit can speak and work the truth. We are given new eyes to see the kingdom of God and to live in light of His truth. We have His Spirit that brings us into His kingdom, so that we may live in proclamation of our new birth.

The Secret of New Birth

Jesus told the Jews *who believed in Him*, "If you abide (continue) in my word, you are truly my disciples, and you will know the truth, and the truth will set you free." John 8:31-32

Their faith was not a saving faith, (the power of the new birth). They were still blind to the truth that was in Jesus. He told them that they would know the truth and be set free from their blindness and the power of sin **if they continued in the truth** that Jesus was speaking to them. We cannot have true faith in something we do not know. We cannot truly know Jesus Christ, who came to bear witness of the truth, unless we continue in God's Word. He has graciously provided and preserved the truth through The Holy Bible for us to know the truth; for us who are His people, to be set free from blindness and sin; that we may **see and enter** into the glory of His kingdom.

If we continue in God's Word the Spirit of truth will convict us of our sin, enable us to understand our blindness, our helplessness; and the need for salvation. The *power of the gospel* works in this new heart and spirit for our regeneration, so that we can in faith turn in repentance from our darkness and the old life of sin and misery, to Christ.

A Conception and Birth of Love

We cannot speak of new birth ~ a spiritual birth that is wrought in the hearts of men ~ as a work that man can claim as any of his own. Just as we cannot conceive or birth ourselves to this human life, neither can we conceive of a new life spiritually. It must be a supernatural act of God and only God.

But, more importantly, we must see it as an act of God's love. It is a father whose seed is planted that sires a natural child. It is the heavenly Father who plants the seed of His own Word, His divine word of Christ, into the hearts of His own children. Let's look at this work of His own love working through His Word and Spirit to produce this new birth.

A Penetrating Love

The writer of the letter to the Hebrews speaks of the power of God's Word; *living and active, sharper than any two-edged sword, piercing to the division of soul and of spirit, of joints and of marrow, and discerning the thoughts and intentions of the heart.* (Hebrews 4:12) Here is the penetrating power of God's love (the seed of His Word) that He alone can plant wherever He wants it.

The wind blows where it wishes (where God wishes) *and you hear its sound, but you do not know where it comes from or where it goes. So it is with everyone who is born of the Spirit.* John 3:8

     The power of God's love is where and when He plans for it to be.

A Love That Permeates and Reshapes the Heart

Where it penetrates, it permeates, saturates, and reshapes, *because God's love has been poured into (spread abroad, KJV) our hearts through the Holy Spirit who has been given to us.* Romans 5:5

In this was manifested the love of God toward us, because that God sent his only begotten Son into the world, that we might live through him. Herein is love, not that we loved God, but that he loved us, and sent his Son to be the propitiation for our sins. 1 John 4:9-10

God shows us His love for us in that while we were still sinners, Christ died for us. Romans 5:8

A Perpetuating Love

The love of God penetrates, permeates and perpetuates His Word in and through us forever. Neither he, nor anyone else will stop this love, or take it away. (Romans 8:38)

But God, being rich in mercy, because of the great love with which he loved us, even when we were dead in our trespasses, **made us alive together with Christ.** Ephesians 2:4-5

According to his great mercy, He has **caused us to be born again to a living hope** *through the resurrection of Jesus Christ from the dead.* 1 Peter 1:3
You have been **born again**, *not of perishable seed but of imperishable,* **through the living and abiding word of God;....** *for the word of God remains forever.* 1 Peter 1:23, 25

We continue in His Word that has given us new life. The same word and power that gives us new life is the same truth that sustains us and enables us to grow and mature. From our justification in Christ (Romans 5:1) we continue in sanctification until we are fully glorified *in the day of redemption.*

Whoever believes in the Son of God has the testimony in himself. 1 John 4:10

Unlike our physical birth, the experience of our new birth is something that we cannot forget, but we continue to speak of it. Through our witness God brings others to His Word and freedom in the truth of Christ. Those who love us, others who are born of His Spirit, rejoice with us. We love to hear their experiences of new life and living *by the Spirit.* We rejoice together and worship the heavenly Father who desired us and sired us through His Spirit and His Word. He keeps us and teaches us, in and of His kingdom here, preparing us to share His glory in eternity to come.

Proof of New Birth

Proof of a new birth will be seen as we *grow in grace and knowledge of our Lord Jesus Christ.* Physical life does not stop after we are born. We are not left in a crib the rest of our lives. We are fed, and we grow and develop into adulthood. And so, our new birth in Christ will show the signs of the nature and disposition of Christ in us (the restored image) as we grow in our relationship with Him.

People who say they are Christian, who stay where they are and have no desire to live for Christ and continue in His word, deceive themselves. Prayer and baptism are only the beginning of the new life. Baptism is an initial, one-time thing.

Prayer is only the beginning of a life of communion with our heavenly Father, through the knowledge of His Word, and intercession of His Holy Spirit.

We are never the same afterward, but in repentance and faith turn from our former way of life, continuing to pray, read, study, memorize and meditate on the truths of God's Word. We desire to know and love Him more; to please Him in all things; we love the things He loves; we serve and worship Him above all things.

Some Christians say that they cannot tell you the day or time of their new birth; but they know that their life is not the same; that God has drawn them to Christ, and brought them to faith and repentance. (Romans 2:4) They have not turned back, (Hebrews 10:38-39) but have continued to walk with Him and to grow in their relationship with Him (2 Peter 3:18).

The new birth, with the new heart, brings us to God's Word for the instructions that He has set forth for His people and His kingdom. Our applying ourselves to know, believe and obey is part of His work in us, for our pattern of life so that we can say, *I know whom I have believed, and am persuaded that he is able to keep that which I have committed unto him against that day.* (2 Timothy 1:12 KJV) The ESV translation says, *which has been entrusted to me.* This carries more weight, since it is His work that has given us this new life and sustains it in us.

> *Let not the foe of Christ and man*
> *this holy seed remove.*
> *But give it root in every heart*
> *to bring forth fruits of love*

(Genesis 3:1-8; Genesis 6:5; Titus 3:1-7; John 16:13; Matthew 7:20; James 1:18, 22; James 2:22; 1 Peter 1:3-8; 21-25 ; 1 Peter 2:9-10; Colossians 1:12-14)

Chapter 3

To Transform ~ *Sanctification*

Do not be conformed to this world,
but be transformed by the renewal of your mind,
that by testing you may discern
what is the will of God,
what is good and acceptable and perfect.
Romans 12:2

When we are in God's Word, we may say that we are "in the know." We are in the only place that God can speak to us, to reveal Himself, and what He wants us to know. The Word is God's means, by the power of the Holy Spirit, through reformation of faith and repentance in us, to *seek the kingdom of God and His righteousness.*

The new heart's desire is to follow in *obedience of faith* in all that God commands of us. We realize, even after regeneration, that we are still unable to

obey, as we should.   We are but babes in Christ
waiting for the food and drink that makes us grow in
our faith. As we continue to study we find more and
more that is required of us.   It may seem that our
obedience is more difficult instead of being easier.
What we discover is that the desires of our hearts and
minds were totally against and unlike God's.   We
must remember that God's kingdom, His nature, His
desires, His righteousness are totally radical to man's.
What God expects from His creatures is more than
we are ever able to do.   But, what He commands of
us, He promises to fulfill in us.

As a child grows physically to maturity, so the
new heart grows as it continues to feed on God's
Word.   As we grow we see more that He has
promised to do.   As that *tree planted by the rivers of water,*
bearing its fruit in its season we too, will continue to grow
and bear the fruit of His Word in due season, as the
vinedresser tends to His own word in us.   He does
not expect anymore than He is able to do in and
through us.

In Romans 12:1 Paul says, "I appeal to you
therefore, brothers, by the mercies of God, to present
your bodies as a living sacrifice, holy and acceptable
to God, which is your spiritual worship."

The mercy he speaks of is the same mercy by
which He *informs* us and *reforms* us.   We are to respond
to His mercy by giving back to Him what He has
given to us.   Our bodies have been made *holy and*
acceptable to God through Jesus Christ's sacrifice for us.
Because He has made His body a sacrifice in dying
for our salvation, we are to consecrate our bodies (all
that we are) to live sacrificially for Him.   We first see

His work in bringing us to faith and repentance; and then in consecration to Him for His continued work on our behalf and for His glory.   It is in this responsive state of a *spiritual worship* that He can continue with His work.   This work through His Word is the only means to bring us from being conformed to the world to a full restoration.

Propensity and Affinity

We have the propensity, the leanings of the sinful nature of the flesh, to continue to be conformed to the world.   For these we need not make any effort. Transformation requires the *renewing of our mind;* and is His working when we give all to Him, so that our new life has an affinity with His Word. His kingdom and His righteousness become ours.

Christ loved the church and gave himself up for her, that he might sanctify her, having cleansed her by the washing of water with the word, so that he might present the church to himself in splendor, without spot or wrinkle or any such thing, that she might be holy and without blemish.   Ephesians 5:25-27

Christ's purpose, in His love for the church (the body of Christ; the household of faith) was to *give Himself for her.*   He died for her, and brings each member of His church, through revelation and regeneration, that He might sanctify her.   How? ~ by *cleansing her by the washing of water with the word.*   Here again is the authority of His Word and the power of His Holy Spirit working to cleanse the heart and mind with the truths of His Word.   He first sets us apart through regeneration unto Himself.   This is our new birth by His Spirit. Then, He sets about, by drawing us to Him for our consecration to him, and the renewing of our minds. We are betrothed to Him, and become one with Him in His love and obedience to the Father.

In teaching my grandchildren this concept of transformation we took a bottle of clear water, symbolizing the heart and mind of man before man sinned, then added dirt and other stuff. We then poured clear water into the bottle until all the other particles had been flushed out. This was an example of how God uses His Word to cleanse and purify what He has set apart for Himself.

And now I commend you to God and to the word of his grace, which is able to build you up and to give you the inheritance among all those who are sanctified. Acts 20-32

Transformation and sanctification continue as long as we are here in the flesh, for we will never be completely transformed to the perfect image of Christ until we pass from this life into His glory. Paul explains this process in the next chapter.

Let not the world's deceptive cares
the rising plant destroy.
But let it yield a hundredfold
with fruits of peace and joy.

(John 17:27; 1 Peter 1:1-2, 4-7; 10:25; 2:1-5; Ephesians 5:25-27; Colossians 1:9-10; Colossians 3:10; 12-17; Hebrews 2:10-12; 1 Corinthians 6:9-11; Acts 26:18)

Chapter 4

To Conform ~ *Glorification*

And we all, with unveiled face,
beholding the glory of the Lord,
are being transformed into the same image
from one degree of glory to another.
2 Corinthians 3:18

The stark and amazing difference in our transformation from our deformed state to the image of Christ does not happen overnight. Even in Jesus' personal teachings for His disciples through His three years with them, He said that they could not bear all things at one time. The human nature is not able to take in or understand divine knowledge and its power of transformation except by degrees; it comes bit-by-bit, precept upon precept.

Paul wrote to the Roman Christians of *the power of the gospel* for faith and salvation that God alone could work. His purpose in writing this letter was to show the effect of the Holy Spirit through the gospel in bringing believers to the "obedience of faith."

We are continually being *transformed* by the renewing of our minds as He, through His Word and Spirit, *conforms us to the image of Christ, His Son.* (Romans 12:1-2 and 8:29) This transformation from one degree of glory to another is to fulfill God's purpose. The great purpose and the planning for our reformation and transformation is explained in Romans 8:28-29.

And we know that for those who love God all things work together for good, for those who are called according to his purpose. For those whom he foreknew he also predestined to be **conformed to the image of his Son**, *in order that he might be the firstborn among many brothers.*

From the distortion of His image in the garden, through Adam and Eve, He reveals His plan from the beginning to conform His people (those He would bring to faith in His Son) to the image of Jesus Christ. Through His birth into our humanity He would be the means of bringing a remnant of His creatures to the Father. Christ is the mediator, through His Work of perfect obedience and righteousness, having fulfilled all requirements of the law, and having received the punishment that we deserve. He is not only our role model, but also the one with power to bring us in obedience to receive His righteousness. He is the means of our justification, our redemption, our adoption and sanctification. Through Him we receive all the benefits that are His to give. In the same written word we are *informed*, *reformed*, brought to faith and repentance, to the process of being *transformed* and *conformed* to the image of Christ. He is the *image of the invisible God; the brightness of His glory; the express image of the Father*. Hebrews 1:3

The Will of the Father

It was the will of the heavenly Father to send His Son to die for His people. (Matthew 1:25) Jesus said that He came to do "the will of Him who sent Him." Since He finished His work here, and ascended back to the Father, His Spirit now is working in all His people to bring them in reconciliation to the Father.

We learn through our study what the will of the Father is for each of us. In our relationship to Christ we are restored to the Father with the new nature and desire to obey and please Him. This is only the beginning of this relationship. It grows through our knowledge of Him as we wait for the *new heavens and the new earth* that He promises.

"But grow in the grace and knowledge of our Lord and Savior Jesus Christ. To him be the glory both now and to the day of eternity. Amen." 2 Peter 3:18

The New Nature

Our study is meant to prepare us for our new state in eternity with the Father and His Son, Jesus Christ. The old nature does not fit with the kingdom of God. His kingdom of righteousness is meant for those whom He has saved in Christ, who are being conformed to His image, making us compatible. You may say that some have been saved on their deathbeds. I will not argue with this. Each of us must answer and be prepared as He effectually calls us, revealing Himself to us. We follow His calling personally, without judging His work in others. We are called and trained through His Word and Spirit to be servants, not judges. He is the only judge. We must answer to Him for what He gives us in our own hearts and lives.

Curtains and Stages

Life as we experience it here on earth has been described in many ways. Some say, "life is a journey." Others describe it as "a path." I, like some, have experienced life "as a theater." It has had its different settings, in different locations, with its plots and characters. God has continually been working to reveal Himself and life as He means it to be by successive action, through His Word and the power of His Holy Spirit. Sitting in darkness, first as a spectator, the curtain of God's Word opened and I watched the action on stage. This has happened many times during my years of Bible study.

In reading and grasping a certain truth from God's Word my thoughts were captured. My mind with a vivid imagination took these thoughts with me everywhere I went. Without knowing when or where, my position changed, from being a spectator in the audience to being in the middle of the action on stage. This was never my doing, but the power of the Holy Spirit working His truths in me.

Christ in you, the hope of glory, is the mystery Paul spoke about in Colossians 1:27. God's Word in us does the work for and through us. This is the power of His Word in us.

The last curtain opened to me was of heaven, where *Christ is sitting on the right hand of the Father, ruling and reigning in glory and majesty, dominion and power,* with the multitude of angels. I, through my imagination, have watched this scene from a distance, and continue to think of this last act, but there are times when I sense that I am part of this cast, caught up in His glory with the angels. This has been His gift to show me what is to come in our knowledge of Him, of His love and grace.

Meditation and Memorization

"There are texts of Scripture which are made and constructed on purpose to make us think. By this means, among others, our heavenly Father would educate us for heaven—by making us think our way into divine mysteries. Hence he puts the word in a somewhat involved form to compel us to meditate upon it before we reach the sweetness of it." Charles Spurgeon

What is the difference between reading, study, meditation and memorization?

Let's think back on the purpose of any other quest for knowledge. A doctor does not become a doctor simply by reading a textbook. There must be much study, memorization, and practice.

A Christian (the common name for those who believe in Jesus Christ) does not become a Christian just by agreeing with what someone says about Christ. Even occasional study does not produce the fruits of Christ. As we stated earlier, it is God's inspired Word through the supernatural working of His Holy Spirit that produces the fruit.

To get the full imprint of God's Word upon our hearts and minds, so as to make us what God intends for us to be, we must take the time to meditate on the Scriptures. This is what we give ourselves to when we present our bodies to Him as a sacrifice. On that altar we desire a full impression of the seed of His Word. For it to take root requires more than a casual reading or study on particular precepts.

Meditation on God's Word is not like any other. There are many who believe in Jesus Christ, but practice other meditations, including Transcendental Meditation and Yoga.

These are practices that require nothing from God, but only a mantra of one word of another god, or breathing techniques that absorb the mind and spirit. Both are derived from another religion.

Meditation on God's Word has no appeal to the average believer. People seek freedom and peace through many different means. I was involved in TM when I was younger and it works, if all you want to do is become your own god and fulfill your own agenda.

Jesus said, "You are my disciples if your continue in my word; and you will know the truth, and the truth will set you free." To continue in His

Word means that it becomes our main thought. To meditate on God's law according to Psalm 1 is a night and day process of remembering who God is as our creator and redeemer, our Father, and who we are as God's children.

The Word Takes Root

"Many of the veils which are cast over Scripture are not meant to hide the meaning from the diligent but to compel the mind to be active, for oftentimes the diligence of the heart in seeking to know the divine mind does the heart more good than the knowledge itself. Meditation and careful thought exercise us and strengthen the soul for the reception of the yet more lofty truths." Charles Spurgeon

Meditation on one reference so that it is seeded and takes root is worth more than just reading through a devotional passage. This is the time that we lie down in green pastures, and sit by the still waters, pondering what the Lord has revealed to us. Memorization can take place before or during meditation, but either way, it is the means of carrying God's truth with us during all times of the day, and as we lie down to sleep at night. The tree that is planted by rivers of living water absorbing God's Spirit and His Word will yield the fruit of what He has planted, in our thoughts, words and actions.

Hear, Hide, and Heed

These are simple words that I taught my grandchildren. We first **hear** and are drawn to what God has spoken to us in His Word. We then **hide** it in our hearts, through memorization and meditation. As it becomes part of us we are continually reminded of what He has spoken by His Spirit within our spirit to **heed** what has been impressed on our minds and hearts.

Meditation is the art of hiding God's Word in our hearts, so that we do not intentionally sin against Him.   (Psalm 119:11) Our minds are naturally disposed to the things of the flesh and the world; we need to understand the battle between the new spirit within us and the flesh, so that by His Word we are prepared to deal with temptation.

The consecration to God's Word that we speak of is first seen as a great need for every Christian.   Understanding the need makes us aware that we are lacking in our devotion to the Lord, but this is meant to bring us with the desire of our hearts, in prayer and supplication to ask for His working in us, so that He teaches us how to study; how to hear; how to hide His Word in our hearts, and by His Spirit, to heed what we read and hear.

Musings or Amusements

How long it takes for meditation of God's Word to become a natural part of our lives depends on what He has to do to bring us to lose ourselves in His Word.   We are so used to the amusements of the world that He has to loose us from those things in which we have been spending our time.   It is so easy to spend hours at a theater, a ball game or other amusements.   We can simply saturate our minds and hearts watching a television screen or whatever we find on the web. The word "web" describes the concept of setting our minds to receive whatever flashes before us. Our minds become entangled with things we watch and hear. This is counteracting the work of His Spirit within our heart and spirit. We will spend our time with what we love, whether the things of God, or the things of the world. While we are being amused, we are missing the beauty and delights of God and His kingdom. Our musings should be on what He loves, and we can only know what He loves by studying His Word; desiring Him to teach us how to love as He loves. His desire for us is, "Let Me entertain you." His garden, His beauty, His landscape is drawn within our hearts and minds in our musings of Him and His Word. He produces the fruit of His Spirit in and through us as we meditate on Him and His truths. We sometimes wonder why life is so difficult; why our circumstances are hard to bear, but He teaches us that He is able to take care and handle all that we face in this life.

Jesus said, "Come unto me, all ye that labour and are heavy laden, and I will give you rest. Take my yoke upon you, and learn of me; for I am meek and lowly in heart: and ye shall find rest unto your souls. For my yoke is easy, and my burden is light." Matthew 11:28-30

Filled with the Holy Spirit through meditation on God's truth, we receive comfort when needed, sufficient strength in our weakness, and peace in times of chaos. No other entertainment or amusement can do this. When faced with trials in this life we can draw on His storehouse of provisions, rather than our reaching for outward means of coping that do not really meet our needs. Our minds remain free and clear in every circumstance that we face because God, in and through His Word is present with us.

"A Bible that's falling apart usually belongs to someone who isn't." C. H. Spurgeon

Remembering the Promises

One thing to begin with in meditation is the category of His promises. As we read we look for these. We stop and contemplate what each one means, studying to whom, when and why the promise was made. Is this a promise for me, or just to a certain person or people? When would this promise be used in my thoughts, my words, and actions? We will look at the practice of meditation and memorization later.

Oft as the precious seed is sown
your quickening grace bestow;
That all whose soul the truth receives
its saving power may know.

(Psalm 73:22-26; Galatians 4:19; Ephesians 4:17-24; Colossians 3:1-4; James 1:22-25 1 Peter 1:6-7; 2:21-25; 1 Peter 4:12-14; 5:10-12)

Chapter 5

To Perform ~ Proclamation

*But what does it say? "The word is near you,
in your mouth and in your heart"
(that is, the word of faith that we proclaim);
because, if you confess with your mouth
that Jesus is Lord
and believe in your heart
that God raised him from the dead,
you will be saved.
For with the heart one believes and is justified,
and with the mouth one confesses and is saved.*
Romans 10:8-10

God, through His Word and His Holy Spirit, has done all the previous work ~ *informing, reforming, transforming, and conforming* us, so that He may *perform* His own work through us. The process is as the seed is planted in fertile soil, germinates, takes root and growing, pushes through the soil upward to the light, and continues to grow and bear fruit.

The fruit of a true Christian comes from within the seed of God's Word planted in the fertile heart, the fruit of God's own holiness and righteousness that is revealed in His Word. This fruit is seen and heard by the proclamation from the mouth of those who hear, read, and know the God who planted the seed of His own Word. By the power of His own Spirit He waters and brings forth the fruit of that seed, the image, the nature, and disposition of His own Son, Jesus Christ; and all to His own glory. This fruit and this proclamation are not just for our own working, but also in all who are plants in His garden. God brings His people together as one, which we know as the church, the body of Christ.

For we are his workmanship, created in Christ Jesus for good works, which God prepared beforehand, that we should walk in them. Ephesians 2:10

Being confident of this very thing, that he which hath begun a good work in you will perform it until the day of Jesus Christ: Philippians 1:6

We see the proof of God's working as each one succeeds in the good work that each one does according to His will. Jesus spoke of some who would be counterfeits. There is no plastic fruit, and no plastic flowers in His garden.

Not everyone who says to me, 'Lord, Lord,' will enter the kingdom of heaven, but the one who does the will of my Father who is in heaven. Matthew 7:21

But be doers of the word, and not hearers only, deceiving yourselves. James 1:22

The Psalmist said: "I have inclined mine heart to perform thy statutes always, even unto the end." Psalm 119:12

The Unity of the Form That God Creates

We imagine this picture of all believers in a certain location uniting together in their individual faith with their gifts of the Spirit, for the same purpose. Let's look at how Paul viewed the church. He spoke of the whole body of believers as being given the fullness of Christ. He died and was raised to give each one of us life in Himself. It was not so that any one would have a higher standing than the other, but that they would bring together the measure that each were given to show the fullness of Christ in the whole body. (Ephesians 1:23)

The fullness of the promised blessings are described in Ephesians 3:16-19. Paul prayed to the Father for the *fullness of God*, the result of the Spirit working in each heart.

So that Christ may dwell in your hearts through faith—that you, being rooted and grounded in love, may have strength to comprehend with all the saints what is the breadth and length and height and depth, and to know the love of Christ that surpasses knowledge, that you may be filled with all the fullness of God.

To "comprehend" is not an individual work on our own, but "with all the saints." Here is the understanding of *the love of Christ that surpasses knowledge*; working in the whole body as each one brings the measure of understanding they have been given, together with all others. No one person is able to understand all, but each part is meant to compliment and add to the other. As the whole body of Christ is involved in the study of God's Word, His Spirit speaks different things to each one, so that they each share and know what they could not have known just as one person. There is no fullness in each one apart from the whole. Things that we may not understand may be explained by what God has given another member of the body.

The Measure Given to Each Member

I therefore, the prisoner of the Lord, beseech you that ye walk worthy of the vocation wherewith ye are called,
2 With all lowliness and meekness, with longsuffering, forbearing one another in love;
*3 Endeavouring to keep the **unity** of the Spirit in the bond of peace.*
*4 There is one body, and one Spirit, even as ye are **called in one hope** of your calling;*
5 One Lord, one faith, one baptism,
*6 One God and Father of all, who is above all, and through all, and **in you all**.*
*7 But **unto every one of us is given grace according to the measure of the gift of Christ**.* Ephesians 4:1-7 KJV

Paul further explains how Christ ascended so that in sending the Holy Spirit He might *fill all things*; and to give leaders to equip the saints for the work of ministry.

(*He who descended is the one who also ascended far above all the heavens, that he might* **fill all things**.)

11 And he gave the apostles, the prophets, the evangelists, the shepherds and teachers,

*12 to equip the saints for the work of ministry, for **building up the body of Christ, until we all attain to the unity of the faith and of the knowledge of the Son of God,** to mature manhood, to the measure of the stature of **the fullness of Christ,***

14 so that we may no longer be children, tossed to and fro by the waves and carried about by every wind of doctrine, by human cunning, by craftiness in deceitful schemes.

*15 Rather, speaking the truth in love, we are to **grow up in every way into him** who is the head, into Christ,*

*16 from whom the whole body, joined and held together by every joint with which it is equipped, when **each part is working properly, makes the body grow so that it builds itself up in love.*** Ephesians 4:10-16

In verse 14 we see the purpose of the knowledge of Christ. Instead of being children, without knowledge, *tossed to and from by every wind of doctrine*, each member of the body of Christ by the Spirit and the Word of God matures and *grows up into Christ*; each part works with the measure of faith and knowledge each is given

"You Know What You Know, and I Know What I Know"

This quote was from our four-year-old granddaughter. Years ago I asked Ansley if their next-door neighbors would be keeping their dog while they were on vacation. She was riding in the back seat of my car, and did not answer when I asked her the first time. Saying that I thought the neighbors might be taking care of their dog since they had done this before, she answered, "Well, you know what you know, and I know what I know."

In shock I almost stopped the car. I did not know how to respond to such a statement from so young a child. She is now a twenty-three-year-old wife and mother, but this experience and her words have remained in my memory. Jerry and I have used this expression through the years, to each other, in response to certain remarks.

I use it here to express that we each are given truths that we share with each other. I may know one thing, but not what you know. I need to listen to what God has revealed through His Word and Spirit to you. We need to listen to each other, with discernment from God's Word and Spirit. Together we will have a bigger picture of God and His kingdom and be a greater and brighter witness to others of the truths of His Word, with more unity and less disagreement. Too, there may, at times, be a need for correction, which can be done in the spirit of grace and love. If we never express what we think to others we may not know that our thinking is wrong. We should, in humility, always be open for correction. It will be a help to future understanding. If we are on a wrong path, in the wrong garden, we may be led further into misunderstanding that prevents our knowing and growing in the truth.

Paul expresses this in his letter to the Philippians.

"Only let your manner of life be worthy of the gospel of Christ, so that whether I come and see you or am absent, I may hear of you that you are standing firm in **one spirit**, with **one mind** striving side by side for the faith of the gospel. "Philippians 1:27

Those who are continually studying God's Word, meditating and memorizing, see the working through each person to bring all to the same mind and spirit, so as to present a true picture of Christ. This needs to be done through the leadership of the church. There must be a central call and theme to the study of certain precepts and books of the Bible so that each one is studying the same passages, and experiencing a unity in thought, word and action.

Christ must be presented as the central character of all God's Word and His church. By faith we are each baptized into Christ, and His body, in the name of the Father, the Son, and the Holy Spirit.

Iron Sharpening Iron

God's Word speaks of *iron sharpening iron.* (Proverbs 27:17) This is in reference to each member of the body through knowledge of God's Word, encouraging each other, challenging each other, exhorting one another.

The writer of Hebrews wrote, "Take care, brothers, lest there be in any of you an evil, unbelieving heart, leading you to fall away from the living God. But exhort one another every day, as long as it is called "today," that none of you may be hardened by the deceitfulness of sin. For we have come to share in Christ, if indeed we hold our original confidence firm to the end." Hebrews 3:12-14

We each need the support and extension of the other members of *the household of faith* to hold each other accountable as to how we represent our Lord Jesus Christ.   Paul likens the church to a physical body where each one is a member of the same body and *through love serves one another.* Galatians 5:13, 6:10

In his letter to the Romans Paul speaks in this way.   "For whatever was written in former days was written for our instruction, that through endurance and through the encouragement of the Scriptures we might have hope.   May the God of endurance and encouragement grant you to live in such **harmony** with one another, in accord with Christ Jesus, that together you may with **one voice** glorify the God and Father of our Lord Jesus Christ. " Romans 15:4-6

Harmony is the unity of all parts in accord with Jesus Christ, so as to be one voice, no one standing out against the other or one that speaks something different than others.

The church stands before the world as an image of Christ; his nature and disposition revealed through the individual members acting in the same spirit and character as the Holy Spirit is working in each heart. The manner of our lives in and out of the church, from one Lord's Day to another, is based on the power of His Spirit working in each heart the truths of God's Word, through each day's study and meditation.   Christ's church is not just a one-day a week fellowship, but of His Spirit continually working His Word in each one. We grow as we continue in His Word. To know Him through His Word is to grow into His image along with other believers who are committed to Christ and His Word.

Divine Power to Destroy Strongholds

In Charles Spurgeon's sermon on "How to Read the Bible" is the reminder that we are disciples of Jesus. If we are truly following Him we will be proclaiming the kingdom of God among the people of the world wherever we are, through the truth of the gospel.

Years ago I was thinking of how we become sentinels, soldiers and good Samaritans in God's kingdom. Christians are guardians of the faith, and are referred to as *soldiers of the cross*, who are in the world continuing to fight the spiritual battles of His kingdom, while Christ is directing the forces that aid us from His throne in heaven. His instructions remain in effect through every generation, until the Holy Spirit has quickened the hearts of all that are His.

Soldiers are trained so that they are prepared for whatever they encounter. The Holy Spirit is the commander that trains us in God's Word, and brings the word to our minds when we are faced with the battle, whether from inner temptations from our minds, or that which comes from the outside. Military forces are trained for every situation. God, through His Word, trains us for the duty to which He calls us. The strategy and victory are all His until *all enemies are put under Christ's feet*.

In striving side by side, in the faith of the gospel, we bind up the wounds of those who are injured in battle; as sometimes we too are recipients of love and care from others.

God's Word ~ the Basis of Truth

Paul instructed Timothy for his duty, that he would be approved for his work. We are not all elders in the church, but soldiers on the battlefield everyday. We will die at the hands of the enemy if we are not prepared.

"Do your best to present yourself to God as one approved, a worker who has no need to be ashamed, rightly handling the word of truth." 2 Timothy 2:15

"But even if you should suffer for righteousness' sake, you will be blessed. Have no fear of them, nor be troubled, but in your hearts honor Christ the Lord as holy, always being prepared to make a defense to anyone who asks you for a reason for the hope that is in you; yet do it with gentleness and respect." 1Peter 3:14-15

We not only will be blessed (*happy*) not to be afraid, nor troubled when we are face to face with the enemy, but we will be ready with the opportunity to explain our hope to those who see and ask about the power of God's Word and Spirit working in our lives. How could the martyrs have suffered at the stake, except they were completely absorbed in the truths of God's Word, prepared and willing to die for the sake of Christ?

The difference in true believers and those who say they believe is seen in where they place their confidence and make their commitments. A believer is one who is born of the Holy Spirit, filled with the Spirit, led by the Spirit, continually walking by the

Spirit. This all begins through His Word and continues throughout our lifetime here on earth.

Paul, in his letter to the early church spoke of the armor of God that is needed to protect us as we *stand against the wiles of the devil* and the spiritual forces that are against God's people.

The last spiritual object that we hold for our defense is the *sword of the Spirit, which is the Word of God.* It is welded in confidence and assurance before the enemy. He cannot fight against the power of God's Word. Jesus used it when in the wilderness, tempted by the devil, until the devil finally left Him.

Submit yourselves therefore to God. Resist the devil, and he will flee from you. Draw near to God, and he will draw near to you. James 4:7-8

It is in submitting ourselves to God by the power of His Word and His Spirit that we resist the devil. His Word in and spoken through us sends the enemy on his heels.

Chosen and Called to Conquer

"A follower of Christ is radically oriented to a different world." Dr. Charley Chase

These words that I heard recently express the position of those who are called and trained in the warfare of the Christian. At this time in the history of our nation and the world we desperately need to be in constant training, and training our children for persecution that is prevalent in many countries. The Word of God living in our own hearts and lives is the only means of defense against the onslaught that continues against the truth revealed in His Word and for which we live and stand. The antithesis will continue until Christ returns. His Word trains us to endure with hope until His coming, at which time all things will be *united in Him, things in heaven and things on earth.* (Ephesians 1:9-10)

In Paul's letter to the Philippians he explained how God works through His people to be light in the darkness of this world.

"Therefore, my beloved, as you have always obeyed, so now, not only as in my presence but much more in my absence, work out your own salvation with fear and trembling, for **it is God who works in you, both to will and to work for his good pleasure**. Do all things without grumbling or questioning, that you may be blameless and innocent, children of God without blemish in the midst of a crooked and twisted generation, among whom you shine as lights in the world, holding fast to the word of life, so that in the day of Christ I may be proud that I did not run in vain or labor in vain."   Philippians 2:12-16

(Leviticus 20:26; Deuteronomy 30:6; Psalm 22:25-31; Psalm 37:23, 31; Psalm 90:17; Isaiah 9:7; 55:11; Jeremiah 1:12; 11:5; 31:33; 33:14; Ezekiel 36:28; Hosea 11:3-4; Malachi 3:17-18; Luke 1:72; John 6:65; Romans 4:21; 1 Corinthians 6:15, 19-20; 2 Corinthians 6:16-18; 10:4-5; Ephesians 3:7-21; 5:30; Philippians 1:29; 2:1-11; 1 Thessalonians 3:11; Hebrews 10:19-25; Hebrews 11:39-40; 12:18-29)

Chapter 6

Conclusion and Beginning

But his delight is in the law of the Lord,
and on his law he meditates day and night.
Psalm 1:2

Now that we have concluded our thoughts on the purpose of Bible Study let us go on to look at the delight of this practice. It has been said that the Holy Bible is "God's personal instruction book for mankind that can prepare him for eternal life and the triumphant return of Jesus Christ to rule this world as King of kings and Lord of lords."

I believe that it is more than this. God, in His Word provides not only the preparation for another life, but the means in this life to know Him, to glorify Him and enjoy Him now, as a prelude to that glorious eternity with Him. Alluding to the garden in which God began life on this earth, the garden from which our first parents were ejected, let us consider God's written Word as another garden into which He brings us. Though this world is a wilderness, which we must all go through, we find God's Word to be a place that He has provided as a respite for us during our pilgrimage.

We come to this garden through a gate He has prepared for us. He invites us to spend time in this garden with Him.

Enter by the narrow gate. For the gate is wide and the way is easy that leads to destruction, and those who enter by it are many. For the gate is narrow and the way is hard that leads to life, and those who find it are few. Matthew 7:13-14

The Lord is the Shepherd that leads us to this garden. (Psalm 23)

The Wonder and Riches of His Garden

The more time we spend in His Word the more we discover the wealth and riches of our heavenly Father and His kingdom that are found in Him and His Son, Jesus Christ. He reveals the Son through His Word; and His Son reveals Him. (Matthew 11:27) When we read and study we should expect that He is with us.

"He is here with me in this chamber of mine: I must not trifle. He leans over me, he puts his finger along the lines, I can see his pierced hand: I will read it as in his presence. I will read it, knowing that he is the substance of it,—that he is the proof of this book as well as the writer of it; the sum of this Scripture as well as the author of it. Lord, be present here; then will I look up from the book to the Lord; from the precept to him who fulfilled it; from the law to him who honoured it; from the threatening to him who has borne it for me, and from the promise to him in whom it is "Yea and amen."   Charles Spurgeon

Buried Treasure

As a child I had a recurring dream of walking a dirt path, and seeing the reflection of the sun on something in the dirt. Reaching down I discovered a penny. (When I was a child we picked up lost pennies.) As I picked it up, I found other pennies. Picking up the pennies, I found nickels underneath, and then dimes, and quarters and half-dollars in the dirt. The more I picked up the more I found buried in the dirt.

I could not understand this dream until the Lord, in my adult life, brought me into His Word. Then, I began to understand the treasures that are hidden there. The more we take the more we see and desire and receive. As we continue to look to the path, and take what He gives, more of the riches of God's covenant and kingdom are revealed.

Jesus said, *It is the Father's pleasure to give you the kingdom* (Luke 12:32). It is His pleasure to open these treasures through His Word, that we may know the heritage that is ours.

In 1993 a year after my *new birth*, I began writing what our heavenly Father was teaching me of our inheritance through Jesus Christ. (1Peter 1: 3-4) I began writing a little book called *The Legacy*. It speaks of a will written by an ancestor who wanted to bequeath His fortune to future descendants.

The Legacy speaks of itself through me, of how God was revealing His love and kingdom to His children who would be born of His Spirit.

God's Word is such as a father would write in His own written will to pass on all the wealth that he has to his children. Those who read and study, meditate, and take to heart in faith what is written, will discover that this wealth is indeed meant for them individually and corporately with other members of the household of faith ~ those whom God births into His own family. He desires us and sires us according to His own will and His timing, in different generations. He brings us through His Word and Spirit to know Him, to be born of Him, to believe and repent, turning in faith to receive all the promises of His inheritance, and to live the abundant life that is ours through His Son, Jesus Christ. There is no life that can compare to this life. It fulfills God's purpose for our creation and redemption and becomes a delight for us as His children.

> *Delight yourself in the Lord,*
> *and he will give you the desires of your heart.*
> (Psalm 37:4).

As we come to this garden that He has prepared for His children, we find all our delight **in Him**. This is His ultimate purpose. God is our goal. His purpose is to satisfy us to the fullest in Himself. His desires become our desires.

The Path and The Pondering Bench

We do not travel far into this garden before we see a bench situated in a shady area as a shield from the heat of the day, where we may view the beauty that He has prepared there. Here we sit for a while and meditate on parts of His Word that He wants us to remember. These meditations hidden in the heart will be carried with us, when we leave the garden. They will be words of wisdom for the wilderness experiences.

We may walk further onto the garden path to discover more paths and deeper truths that He has waiting for us. These are the "paths of righteousness" by which the Shepherd leads.

Experiencing God's Word With All Our Senses

Our time spent in His Word is God's means of awakening our senses to the things of His kingdom. Living in sin and apart from Him, our senses are dull, they are dead to Him. Our faculties are harnessed by His Spirit, so His Word does all that He wants it to do, in and through us; all for His glory and our joy.

Paul in his letter to the Corinthian church quoted Isaiah when he said, "But, as it is written, 'What no eye has seen, nor ear heard, nor the heart of man imagined, what God has prepared for those who love him'—these things God has revealed to us through the Spirit. For the Spirit searches everything, even the depths of God." 1 Corinthians 2:9-10

Our eyes are opened by the light of His Word. Our ears are opened to hear His voice. We can spiritually touch, taste, and smell the sweet fragrance of His kingdom that is revealed to us in Christ through His Word.

His Word speaks of our being light and salt, and a sweet fragrance of Christ.   Matthew 5:13; 2 Corinthians 2:15

Green Pastures

The Lord is the Shepherd that feeds His sheep, causing them to lie down in green pastures. Here we taste and see that He is good. He has provided the pasture for His sheep to lie down and rest. Here we may also bask in the sun of His love, away from the coldness of the world.

Ponds and Pools of Cleansing Water

The Shepherd leads us by the still waters. There are ponds by which we may sit and enjoy His creation. There are pools in which we may lie down and saturate ourselves. Sometimes we need to soak in His Word to be cleansed. His Word is a purifier for our heart, mind, and soul.

Brooks, Refreshing Springs and Waterfalls

The fountain of wisdom is a bubbling brook. Proverbs 18:4

There are springs whereby our journey's thirst is quenched. Our minds and hearts are prone to take in the sights and sounds of the world. Our Father provides beautiful waterfalls where we may stand and feel the refreshing of His Spirit through His Word and a washing away of the things of this world and the wilderness.

There is not only the beauty of the landscape of flowers, but trees laden with fruit, just waiting to be picked and eaten. There is a vegetable garden, waiting for our nourishment.

There are large rocks with clefts in the rocks in which we find shelter from the lightening and the storm.

When we spend time in His garden every day we have all that we need to face the world, its temptations, its oppressions and its chaos. In this garden we find love, joy, peace and contentment. There is order in this garden according to God's covenant. When we come to His Word for wisdom and knowledge of Him and life, He brings order into our lives even in the middle of the wilderness.

The Seed of the Word

The same word written is the same word that is planted and produces the fruit of the seed. Jesus speaks in a parable about the word as a seed, with the example of four seeds, one falling on a path, never germinating, one on rocky ground, one planted among thorns, and one planted in fertile soil. The only seed that bears fruit is the one planted in fertile soil. God's Word bears its own fruit when planted in a fertile heart. As we spend time in the garden of His Word our new hearts become more fertile for the seed of His Word to germinate and bear its fruit. Here again we can meditate on this verse that we read earlier.

He is like a tree planted by streams of water
that yields its fruit in its season,
and its leaf does not wither.
In all that he does, he prospers.
Psalm 1:3

The seed of His Word will begin to produce His fruit. We shall prosper in what the Word does in and through us. It is the authority of the Word that is commanded in us by the Holy Spirit.

Augustine is quoted as saying, "The Bible was composed in such a way that, as beginners mature, its meaning grows with them."

You may say that you have never experienced this growth or this fruit in your life. Even if you have been an avid student of God's Word, and still do not see the fruit that we speak of, don't give up. It may take years for Him to plow the furrows of your heart. You may learn easily, while in meditation and memorization, but not sense a change in your heart and life at first. The humility that is needed may not come except through difficult times. The times that you spend in adversity will not be in vain. You would not be in His Word except He calls you there. His Word will stand the testing over time. It is only in this, as His Word to us personally, that we are to trust. It is the authority in all things, especially in reforming our hearts and lives.

Water for the Soul

And the LORD will guide you continually and satisfy your
desire in scorched places and make your bones strong; and you

shall be like a watered garden, like a spring of water, whose waters do not fail. Isaiah 58:11

We can't plant a garden in our own hearts. Just as we cannot create ourselves, we can't reform our own hearts; the work has to be His alone. We simply follow through His Word looking for and claiming the promises that are revealed. A seed does not germinate overnight, nor grow to its full potential in our timing. This work in our souls is supernatural, but occurs as we continue to look to Him in His Word for what He promises.

It is soul work, as Jeremiah prophesied, "Therefore they shall come and sing in the height of Zion, and shall flow together to the goodness of the Lord, for wheat, and for wine, and for oil, and for the young of the flock and of the herd: **and their soul shall be as a watered garden**; and they shall not sorrow any more at all." *Jeremiah 31:12 KJV*

As I am writing this and considering the magnitude and the magnificent work of God's creation and redemption, of His preparation of a people who will share His glory, I imagine this realm of the knowledge of God to be one of absorption. A garden employs every element to make it one unique landscape. So, we consider the heart and soul, the seed and fruit in the gardener's hand. He joins all together, His Word taking shape within us. As we are living in His garden of knowledge we become a part of it; we, in His Word, and His Word taking shape within us.

Crown Him the Lord of peace,
whose power the scepter sways.
From pole to pole that wars may cease,
absorbed in prayer and praise.

This is the result of the Lord working His Word and knowledge in us. Whether we think of the triangle in Chapter 1 as a wide road that narrows toward the source and point of the light, or a mountain with a pinnacle to be reached, we may realize this area as the sanctity of God that he has provided for those whom He is drawing to Himself by His Spirit and Word; those who know and love Him and continue to seek Him.

It is in this sanctuary that His Word and Spirit continue to inform us, reform us, keep us, and prepare us throughout this life for eternal life with Him.

"The Church of Christ, whose heart is a garden and her graces as precious spices, prays for the heavenly breathings of the Spirit, that her sacred spices might flow out."
Thomas Watson ~ *The Art of Divine Contentment*

The Eternal Paradise

The garden is a taste of what is to come in our inheritance. God began His creation in a garden, and will consummate all things in that celestial city to which He is leading us. The garden of His Word reminds us that the wilderness is only temporary. His plans to bring us to an eternal paradise will not fail.

Our hope is given through His Word, and keeps us in hope and faith until He brings us home to be with Him and all His other children.

When we leave the garden to venture on through the wilderness we carry what He has given. We hide it in our hearts and take it with us.

It is our weapon of defense for all that would assault us. We are prepared for the enemy who waits at every turn. When we speak the Word he flees and we go on in praise to our Lord and Savior, who through His Word and Spirit are always with us.

Thy Word is Like a Garden, Lord

Thy Word is like a garden, Lord,
With flowers bright and fair;
And every one who seeks may pluck
A lovely cluster there.
Thy Word is like a deep, deep mine;
And jewels rich and rare
Are hidden in its mighty depths
For every searcher there.

Thy Word is like a starry host:
A thousand rays of light
Are seen to guide the traveler,
And make his pathway bright.
Thy Word is like an armory,
Where soldiers may repair,
And find, for life's long battle day,
All needful weapons there.

O may I love thy precious Word,
May I explore the mine,
May I its fragrant flowers glean,
May light upon me shine
O may I find my armor there,
Thy Word my trusty sword;
I'll learn to fight with every foe
The battle of the Lord.
Amen.

Edwin Hodder 1863

Chapter 7

Process and Results

All these things my hand has made,
and so all these things came to be,
declares the LORD.
But this is the one to whom I will look:
he who is humble and contrite in spirit
and trembles at my word.
Psalm 66:2

The best process for Bible study is in union with your local church. The church, wherever it meets locally consists of members who have been baptized into the body of Christ. Pastors should be leading the flock that has been assigned to them by bringing each one into a chosen study of one of the books of the Bible. This is the means of unity in the whole body; as each member studies, learns the truths, and joins in like mind and spirit to portray the image of Christ that is seen there. Ask your pastor about this. Many churches have Bible study classes within a set period of time when they meet on the Lord's Day. **The effective studies are those that involve each person's home study, preparation and sharing what they have learned.** These are separate than the expository preaching done by the pastor in the Lord's Day worship service.

The other study recommended is with the head of each household leading the family. This too should be related to what the whole church is studying.

Until there is a Bible study in your church in which you can participate, commit to your family's study, or study on your own, if you are single. There are many ways to study, meditate and memorize God's Word. You can begin by using a one-year read-through schedule. (See Author page) At some point, this should be done in addition to the study of a particular book of the Bible. Churches should be involved in reading the Bible through every year. Pastors who lead their members in this year-by-year reading can, in their sermons, refer to passages that have been read during the week. It is a joy to hear a Bible reference with which we are familiar used in a sermon. Children become involved in the unity of the church where this is practiced.

Entering the Garden With Prayer

"Now, if we are thus to understand what we read or otherwise we read in vain, this shows us that when we come to the study of Holy Scripture we should try to have our mind well awake to it. We are not always fit, it seems to me, to read the Bible. At times it were well for us to stop before we open the volume. "Put off thy shoe from thy foot, for the place whereon thou standest is holy ground."   As you ask a blessing over your meat, so it would be a good rule for you to ask a blessing on the word before you partake of its heavenly food. Pray the Lord to strengthen your eyes before you dare to look into the eternal light of Scripture. Say to your soul—"Come, soul, wake up: thou art not now about to read the newspaper; thou art not now perusing the pages of a human poet to be dazzled by his flashing poetry; thou art coming very near to God, who sits in the Word like a crowned monarch in his halls. Wake up, my glory; wake up, all that is within me. Though just now I may not be praising and glorifying God, I am about to consider that which should lead me so to do, and therefore it is an act of devotion. So be on the stir, my soul: be on the stir, and bow not sleepily before the awful throne of the Eternal." Scripture reading is our spiritual meal time. Sound the gong and call in every faculty to the Lord's own table to feast upon the precious meat which is now to be partaken of. " Charles Spurgeon

Begin with prayer to seek God's will in how you proceed in this endeavor. What I suggest is a simple means to mine His Word. In one of the studies with my grandchildren we made paper headlights ~ the kind miners wear. This was a means of expressing the need for light as we dig deep into God's Word.

Simple Guideline for Study

We don't need to go overboard when we study. The simple things will progress to greater things. As you mature in your faith the Lord will guide you in your own personal study with Him.

First, remembering that we are looking for God and Jesus Christ as the main characters of His Word, we will see their direction in almost every passage that we read.

There are three points that I used for teaching: *identification, implication and application.*

Identification: There is no story without characters. God, as the Creator, Father, Son, and Holy Spirit, is the main character we look for; but what other characters are included in the passage we are studying? How do they relate to each other? What occurs between these persons, either between them and God or between each other.

Implication: What is implied in what we are studying? What is the purpose of the passage? What is happening in the story?
What is the outcome? What? Where? When? These are questions to ask in what we are studying. What difference does this part of God's Word make in our search for Him and our knowledge of Him and in our own life, our family, our church, the church worldwide, and the world?

Application: How does what we have studied apply to our own lives? Do we see references that speak to our relationship to God? What principles do we see that are applicable to today? What does God want me to learn from this passage? How does what we study affect our relationship with Him and with our spouse, our children, our parents, our siblings, extended family, and the members of our church body, or to those we see each day? What truths do we come away with from our study and meditation?

Remember that the purpose of our study is not just personal, but meant to affect our relationship with the whole body of Christ, of which each of us is a member. When we begin to think of all that we do, as part of "our" relationship with God, the delight of study will come. Remember that study is not just for ourselves, but to bring in our spirits what God gives each of us, *for the edifying of the whole body ~ comprehending with all saints the length, breadth, depth and height of the love of Christ, which is beyond knowledge ~ and so be filled with the fullness of God.* Ephesians 3:18-19

Our study will take on even greater dimensions when we see the effects of our individual studies in the whole body of Christ. This is the purpose of "our" Bible study. It is "our" garden. It is "our" Lord; "our" Father in heaven; "our" Savior, Jesus Christ; "our" Holy Spirit; "our" church. All that each of us is given is to be added to the whole that is "ours" in Christ. It is when we open the gate of God's Word and enter in that we prove we are a part of His kingdom. If we have no interest in what He gives us of His kingdom here, we will have no interest in His kingdom there and for eternity. Fruit comes from the seed that is planted in our hearts here. It flourishes now, but does not come to full bloom until gathered with all others in the new heavens and the new earth. What God plants in each heart is the beginning of our individual reward in heaven.

M&Ms ~ Nourishment for the Soul

Growing deeper and stronger in our relationship with our Creator ~ the writer and by His Spirit, interpreter of His Word ~ comes in our practice of meditation and memorization.

From reading, to study, to mediation, each requires more time and commitment. Here again, we think of the time that we spend with the things that we love, and with what we want to become in this life. If you have spent anytime in the study of a career you understand the process and the results.

Being transformed, and conformed to the image of God happens as we spend time with Him. Learning how to construct our time we will find it to be more fruitful. M&Ms are a favorite candy for children, and adults who are still "children at heart." It doesn't take much time to eat these; simply pop them in your mouth and enjoy. Depending on how long you want them to last you either chew and swallow, or you suck on them until you have removed the outer coating, then suck on the chocolate, or allow it to dissolve in your mouth. There is a similarity between how one consumes physical food and how we process and digest God's Word.

Some don't eat M&Ms. They don't buy them because they don't eat chocolate or sugar, they don't like coatings, or they are just not casual eaters. Similarly, there are people who don't like God's Word. They don't buy it, for many reasons.

And there are those who quickly chew and swallow without too much thought of what they are consuming, while they go about their business. Similarly, there are those who read God's Word, even daily, but chew only as long as it takes to get through the selected passage scheduled for the day.

Then there are some who take time to relish the moments, the taste and the joy of the sugar and chocolate.   Similarly, there are some who sit down with the intentions of getting the most and the longest lasting benefit from God's Word.

At some point the sugar and the chocolate from the M&Ms kick in and do their work. In the same way, memorization and meditation in God's Word have their effect.

Memorization is the outer coating that capsules for our hearts and minds what we want to remember. Meditation is the process of discovering the inner delicacy; it is the means of experiencing more of the hidden truths of God's Word, those that most affect the heart and life.

Fruit of Our Thoughts

What we study and hide in our hearts, continues to affect our thinking, and eventually our actions. The truths of God, of Christ, and the power of His Holy Spirit, are the sugar and chocolate that become a part of our spiritual system, and these activate God's Word in our souls. But, better than candy, God's word provides eternal nourishment.   M&Ms are addictive; and so is meditation in God's Word, once you taste, and know that the Lord is good.

From reading and study, we set our minds and hearts on the seed and the fruit that we find. An example of this process is in my recent musings in *Meditations in Galatians.* My personal study from the letter itself includes knowing the author, Paul, and his purpose for writing to the churches in Galatia. The time frame is early Christianity. Paul is addressing the issue of religion pertaining to the Jewish faith, as different from the new faith, that came in and through the person and work of Jesus Christ. Paul is writing to refute the need of the Gentiles for circumcision. The Judaizers were convincing those of the churches in Galatia that they had to be circumcised, in addition to believing in Christ.

After reading through, studying what Paul was teaching the new Christians in Galatia, we can then go back and look at each chapter. Spending time in the first chapter we pinpoint the most important things that we want to remember.

We already know from our study who the main characters are: Paul, the new believers, and those coming from a Jewish background. We know the implications; the Christians in Galatia are being influenced by the Jews;, and Paul is appealing to them to consider how they came to believe, and not to accept anything more than what he preached to them in the gospel when they first believed. He wants them to know the freedom that they have in Christ, to go on in faith by the same Spirit in which they were brought to faith, and not to get hung up on anything else that they think they have to do.

Our meditations should be established on the references that apply to all time, including our time. We don't have to deal with circumcision, but we still have the same temptations from other sources that teach that something besides our faith in the finished work of Christ is needed for our relationship with God.

With this in mind we look to the first chapter and take away from it what every generation needs to know and remember.

As an example from Galatians 1:3-5 we accept the greeting as if it was to us personally and to our church in this generation. I am using the ESV in my study.

> *Grace to you and peace from God our Father*
> *and the Lord Jesus Christ,*
> *who gave himself for our sins*
> *to deliver us from the present evil age,*
> *according to the will of our God and Father,*
> *to whom be the glory forever and ever. Amen.*

These three verses are enough to consider at one sitting. One visit into the garden will enable us to come away with a joy and delight as we take these words personally to heart. These words and thoughts will relate to the whole context of Paul's letter and to our own lives. I will not tell you how long and how you should meditate on this blessing, but taking each morsel and chewing on it makes it life to us. Saturating our minds in these words transforms our thinking. As we meditate, the mind will almost memorize in its own processing. Or, we can memorize parts and meditate on each phrase. These work together. These become part of our thinking; and the more we think on these things the more they become real in us. From this first part of Paul's letter we venture into the next part that is applicable to this part and what relates to our own thinking and living. God's kingdom is the same from generation to generation, so we find, meditate on and remember those things that pertain to eternal life ~ life in Christ that He came to give.

My prayer for you, dear reader, is that the Spirit of the Father will draw you to His Son, Jesus Christ; to the hidden gate through which you may find this abundant life, and this delight in Him. A day without this time in His garden will prove to be a day lacking in nourishment and joy. It is an endless adventure of which you will never tire, but will find it growing sweeter and more glorious every day.

(See the first in series *What the Bible Says About LIGHT,* a Ten-Week Devotional Study.)

"Oh, cling you to Scripture. Scripture is not Christ, but it is the silken clue, which will lead you to him. Follow its leadings faithfully." Charles Spurgeon

"Now to him who is able to do far more abundantly than all that we ask or think, according to the power at work within us; to him be glory in the church and in Christ Jesus throughout all generations, forever and ever.

Amen."

Ephesians 3:20-21

Final Words

Let the high praises of God be in their mouth,
and a two-edged sword in their hand;
Psalm 149:6 KJV

Let us not leave out of this treatise the reminder that the two-edged sword is the Word of God that brings judgment upon God's creation for its sin and rebellion. Those who, by faith receive the truth of God's Word here, will be saved from His judgment in eternity. We, who are born of His Word and Spirit, carry this two-edged sword with us at all times. It is God's light in us as a judgment upon the world ~ its darkness and decay. Any peace in the world is in and through His written and living Word, spoken and living in us.

"Do not think that I have come to bring peace to the earth. I have not come to bring peace, but a sword."
Matthew 10:34

Christ came to separate the light from the darkness through the truth of His Word spoken by the prophets, the apostles, and all His followers.

To those who heard Jesus speak, He promised love, mercy, grace, and forgiveness, and eternity with Him. He promises to those who would not receive Him and His Words that they will be judged by those words.

"I have come into the world as light, so that whoever believes in me may not remain in darkness. If anyone hears my words and does not keep them, I do not judge him; for I did not come to judge the world but to save the world. The one who rejects me and does not receive my word has a judge; the word that I have spoken will judge him on the last day. For I have not spoken on my own authority, but the Father who sent me has himself given me a commandment—what to say and what to speak. And I know that his commandment is eternal life. What I say, therefore, I say as the Father has told me." John 12:44-50 (See also Revelation 2:16; 19:15, 21)

Gracious Father, as we conclude this work, please use it to your glory, as by your grace you draw your people to your written Word, and to the living Word, Jesus Christ, your dear Son; that we may all know the delight and joy that is ours in you, our eternal Father. We wait in anticipation for that day when He shall return to claim His own. In Jesus' precious name I pray. Amen.

About the Author

Fran Rogers is a wife/caregiver to her husband of 55 years, a 77-year-old great-grandmother, writer and blogger in Buford, Georgia. She writes from the experience of enduring many difficulties while living in the reality of God's grace. Through God's Word she has learned to be dependent on Him for all things, witnessing His love, joy, and goodness. Writing for over twenty-five years, she is now beginning to publish what God has been teaching her. The purpose of publishing is to share with God's people the legacy of His kingdom. She is a witness of God's provisions for all things of this life, and even more; the eternal life that He has prepared for all His people. The majority of proceeds from sales will be given to charity and to missions that witness of God's kingdom throughout this world. In view of Christ's promise that He would have witnesses in *Jerusalem, Judea, and Samaria, and to the uttermost part of the earth,* her hope is that God's people who read will not only benefit, but also promote this message to others through their purchase. See the website fatherandfamily.com for more details of this ministry.

Listed are other works available, soon to be published, or in progress. Most of her writing is included in the series *Little Books About the Magnitude of God*; her work is longer than an article but not as extensive as a regular length book.

Thank you for reading. Please consider posting a review online, so that others may be encouraged to read.

FREE EBOOKS

FIRST THINGS That Last FOREVER

fatherandfamily.com

Sign up for a second free eBook
TWO FULL PLATES ~ Learning to be a Caregiver
www.fatherandfamily.com/free-eBook/

Website: fatherandfamily.com
Blog: godsgracegodsglory.com
Facebook: Father and Family Books
Contact: contact@fatherandfamily.com

You might want to try DISCIPLIESHIP JOURNAL'S Yearly Bible Reading Plan from navigators.org.

Other books in series *Little Books About the Magnitude of GOD*   *((Published *)*

*FIRST THINGS That Last FOREVER
*TWO FULL PLATES ~ Learning to be a Caregiver
*The LITTLE BOAT and other Short Stories of GOD'S GRACE
Child Keeping ~ The Blessing to Parents
Prayers That Brought the House Down
One Month to Live ~ A Father's Last Words
A Broad Review of Andrew Murray's "Humility"

Notes on Paul's Letter to the Romans
Legacy of the Seven Psalms + One
God's Grace ~ God's Glory

Series *What the Holy BIBLE Says*

*What the Holy BIBLE Says About LIGHT
What the Holy BIBLE Says About GOD'S WORD
What the Holy BIBLE Says About LIFE

Other Books
Waiting is Not a Game~ Articles of Faith
My Garden and other Poems of God's Grace

www.ingramcontent.com/pod-product-compliance
Lightning Source LLC
Chambersburg PA
CBHW020511030426
42337CB00011B/328